ENCHANTED FOLKLORE
Coloring

chartwell
books

Gnomes, pixies, sprites, and goblins galore!

id you love traipsing through the woods or making up imaginative stories as a child? Then you'll love everything folklore, where you can celebrate all manner of creatures, great and small.

Whether you're an admirer of gnomes and pixies, sprites and changelings, or fairies and unicorns, there's something for you in *Enchanted Folklore Coloring*. Inspired by myth, legend, and fairytale, enchanted folklore relishes the wonderful diversity of all other-worldly beings, both lovely and frightening. These delightful images are designed to help you get coloring but also to help you explore your own personal creative side.

Just as there is no right or wrong way to use this book, there is no right or wrong way to color. You can color in these curious and charming illustrations however you wish and in whatever way feels right to you. Cool blues, vibrant greens, rich browns, lush purples, it's all up to you! This is about getting in touch with what makes you unique, so if one coloring page doesn't appeal to you, simply move on to one that fits your mood.

One of the great things about coloring is that it's accessible to anyone, regardless of artistic experience. Being able to add your own colors helps make it more personal, and, just like the enchanted creatures themselves, there's no pressure to make these drawings perfect. So turn the page and start your journey!

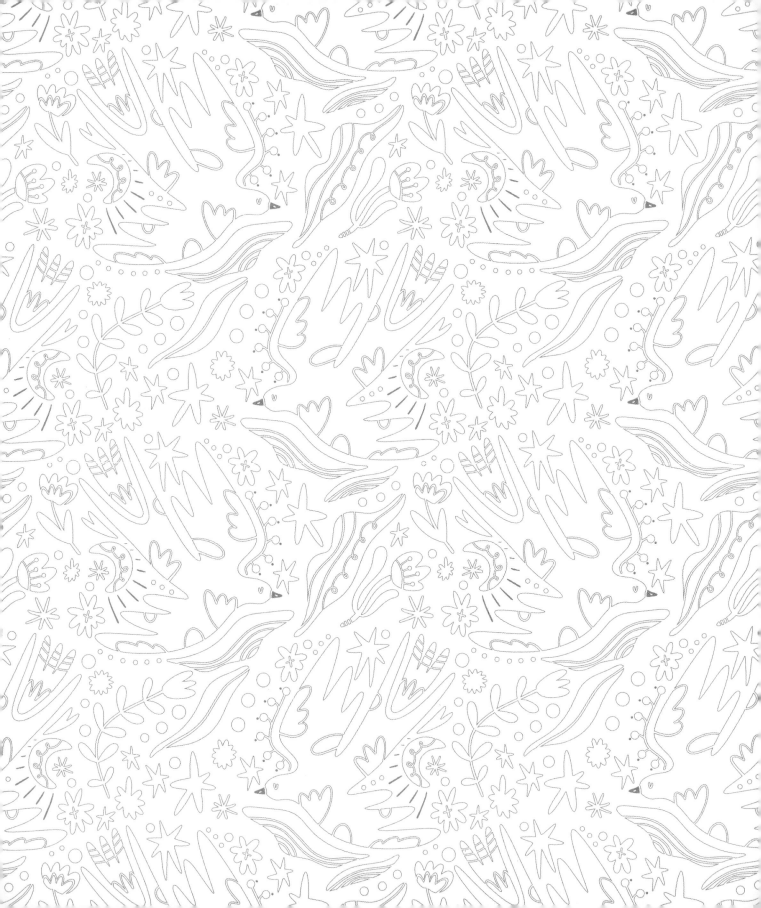

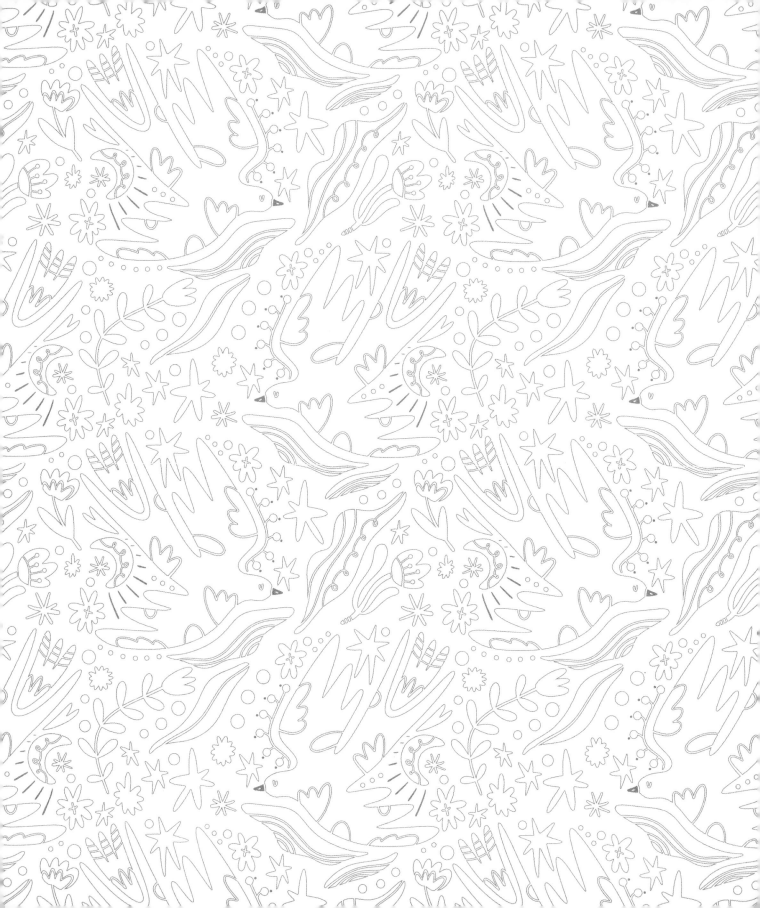

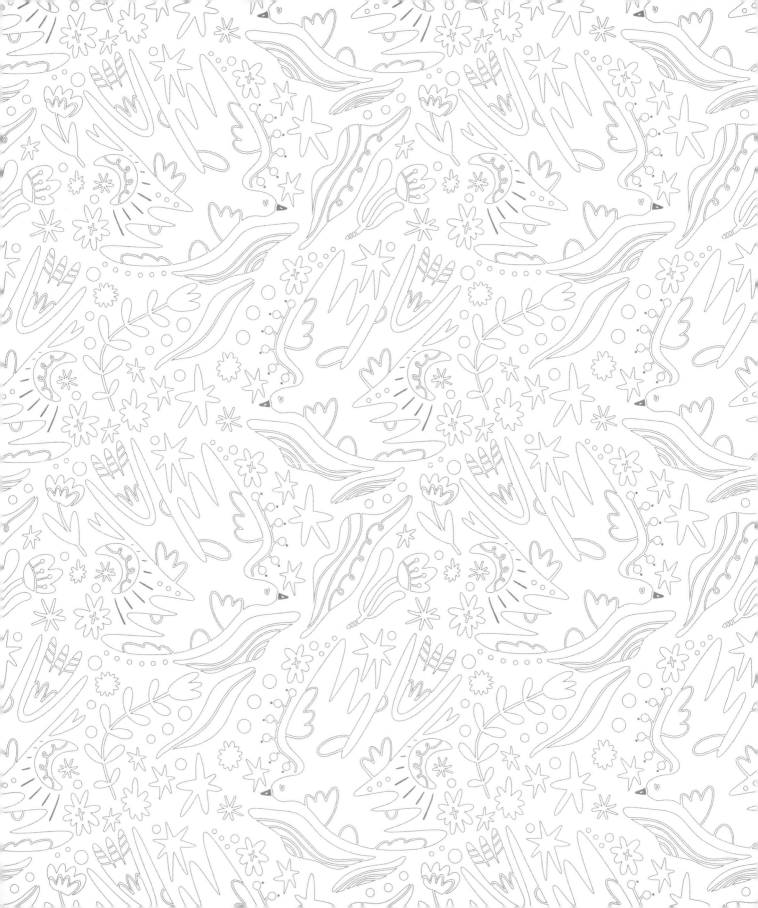

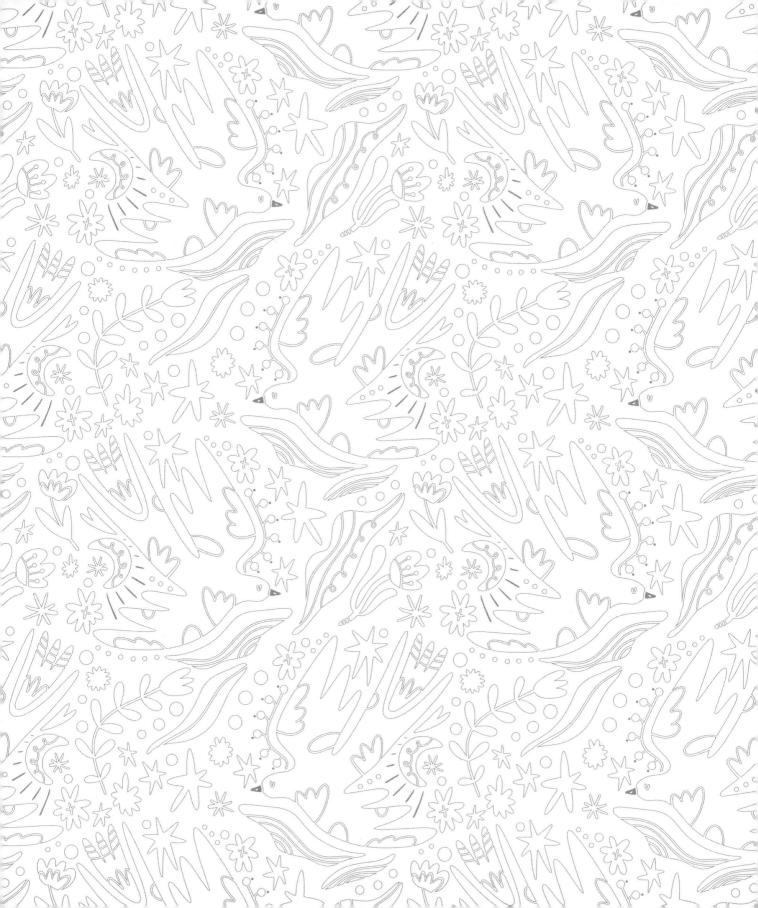

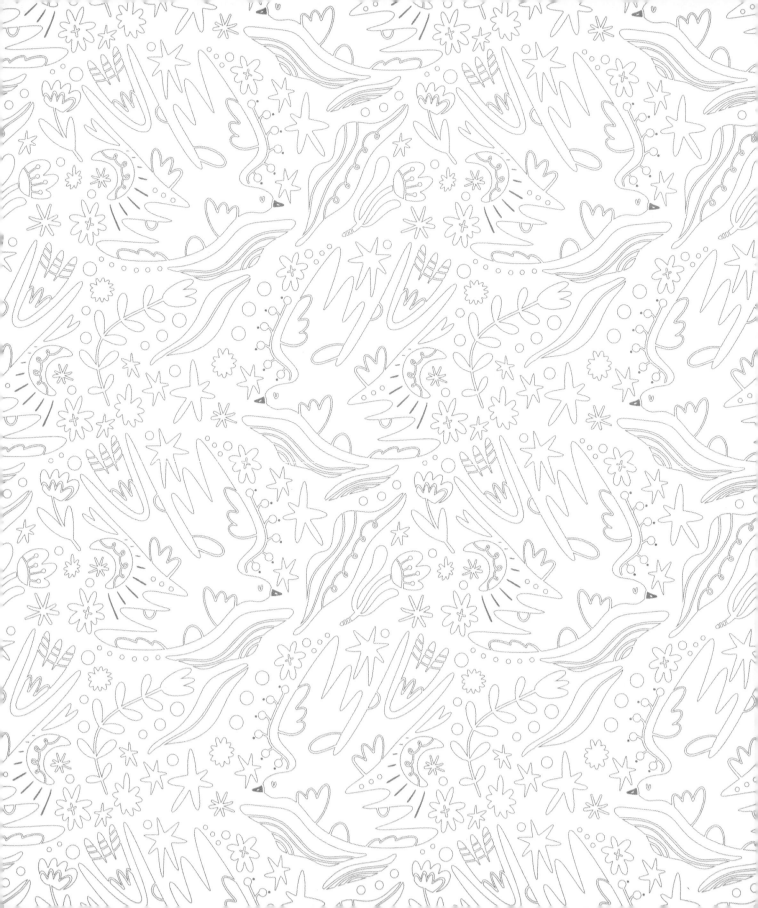

Quarto

This edition published in 2023 by Chartwell Books,
an imprint of The Quarto Group
142 West 36th Street, 4th Floor
New York, NY 10018 USA
T (212) 779-4972 F (212) 779-6058
www.Quarto.com

10 9 8 7 6 5 4 3 2 1

Chartwell titles are also available at discount for retail, wholesale, promotional, and bulk purchase. For details, contact the Special Sales Manager by email at specialsales@quarto.com or by mail at The Quarto Group, Attn: Special Sales Manager, 100 Cummings Center Suite 265D, Beverly, MA 01915, USA.

ISBN: 978-0-7858-4322-1

Publisher: Wendy Friedman
Senior Managing Editor: Meredith Mennitt
Senior Design Manager: Michael Caputo
Cover Designer: Kate Sinclair
Interior Designers: Sue Boylan, Alana Ward
Editor: Jennifer Kushnier
Image credits: Shutterstock

Printed in China